# DESIRING
# FLIGHT

# DESIRING FLIGHT

*Christianne Balk*

PURDUE UNIVERSITY PRESS / WEST LAFAYETTE, INDIANA

99 98 97 96 95    5 4 3 2 1

The paper used in this book meets the minimum requirements
of American National Standard for Information Sciences—
Permanence of Paper for Printed Library Materials, ANSI Z39.48-1984.

Printed in the United States of America
*Design by Chiquita Babb*

*Library of Congress Cataloging-in-Publication Data*
Balk, Christianne
    Desiring flight / Christianne Balk.
        p.    cm.
    ISBN 1-55753-062-9
    I. Title.
PS3552.A4538D47  1995
811'.54—dc20                                94-38209
                                                        CIP

# ACKNOWLEDGMENTS

Grateful acknowledgment is given to the Ingram Merrill Foundation, to the Alaska Council on the Arts, to Andres Berger and Northwest Writers for support which aided in the writing of these poems, and to the following periodicals, in whose pages these poems have first appeared:

*The Bellingham Review:* "Dusk Choir"
*Country Journal:* "John Muir Dreams"
*Crazyhorse:* "Why I Did It"
*Cutbank:* "Stehekin Light," "Separation"
*Jeopardy:* "Distant Cities"
*The New Republic:* "Dear Hippopotamus"
*The New Yorker:* "John Muir Remembers Eliza Hendricks"
*Pequod:* "The Road to Marshfield Lake"
*Ploughshares:* "Departure," "Armistice," "Where the Long, Lazy Mothers Stroll"
*Poetry Northwest:* "Kantishna Terns," "Storm"
*Seattle Times:* "Kantishna Morning"
*Sow's Ear Poetry Review:* "The Breeze Nudges the Junipers, Promising"
*Willow Springs:* "You Say You Love How Unexpected, Open Fields"

"Dusk Sea Walk" was originally published as "Before the Spill: Celebrating the Sea at Dusk (Kenai Peninsula, March 23, 1989)," in *Season of Dead Water,* edited by Helen Frost (Breitenbush Books, Inc. 1990).

Many thanks to Mira Braunstein, Tebby Lavery, Pam Mullens, and Kate Dennis for their support, and to Andrew Hudgins for his help with the final version of this manuscript.

*For Karl and Elizabeth*

# CONTENTS

I

DEPARTURE

# OLD MINTO

Night never comes. Dawn elbows
morning in, shrugs off dusk. I think

of river people hunched in flat-
bottomed boats, tree-anchored, waiting

for the river to recede. Rain rots
timber frames. Snowmelt sags the ceilings. Cabins
slide off poled spruce stilts. I stir

the smudge fire bare-handed, step

into the smoke. Yellow anemones
smolder. The blackflies hum,
carry bits of me away.
Aspens twist, bent by fire. Where are

the flames? Eggs, berries, and roots lie

drenched. Fish baskets tangle
in their own lines. Dip nets float

aimlessly. Pike escape downstream.

Moose wade garnished with flag iris stems
easy in the village green, and slip

unstartled into shadows spun from balsam
poplar to cinquefoil. Leather lashings
come undone. The hands that braided everything

are gone. Old laps rest on the ridge.
Heavy ground, tilled by frost, barely

holds the picket fence stamped with stars
and crosses. From up here, the Minto Flats
stretch as far as I can see

each lake, creek, rill, mire, pond, and bog

named by people whose words
burr like the wings of swans returning

to nest
in the spring, in the rain, in the sun, in the wind, in the sloughs'

exaltations of mosquitoes.

## KANTISHNA TERNS

Arched bodies hovered
over us, wings
beating,
soapstone bellies
shining, scissor tails opening
and closing,
snapping shut,
slicing our fire's smoke.
Sharp, white sticks poised midair.
Their whistles rasped.
We hesitated,
afraid of hidden nests.
The zippers on our sleeping bags
joined together,
one big bag for both of us—
the smell of oilcloth and paraffin.
"Will you?" you asked.
I was too tired to know, but secretly
I asked *forever? What is that?*
All night I heard the sounds
I'd heard all day—
water meeting wood, water
washing dirt,
shore-rushed, rain-roughened river
now whirling in pools, now
smoothing,
reflecting light
the way scrub willows mirror
wind, streaks
of silver quickly moving through,

then passing on.
The snags we saw—
whole trees, some of them.
Each one thrashing
the surface, hooked
to unseen anchors,
struggling. I watched
one branch break free of rock
and begin
to float downstream.

## DUSK SEA WALK

The sky's burnt orange and the sea's burnt orange
streaked with pewter. God, even our faces
glow orange enough right now to make us
talk about another child. Can I hold
my daughter's hand long enough to keep her dry?
Look, she's filled her mouth with beach gravel.
That's right, spit them out in Mommy's hand, every one.
Watch out! The sea takes anything it wants—
stones arced from small hands, needled starfish,
limpets, loaded tankers, the blue and white rush
of breaking ice, northbound flecks of teal, the seiner
we spent all winter scraping and sanding. This sea
wants everything—the black cod's eye, phalarope,
green fucus, milky clouds of milt, the otter's coat,
the shadowed cracks between each rock along this jagged
coast, sooty shearwater and steel-hulled ship,
sea lions thick with pups, razor clams, pot shrimp,
krill, snow crab, barnacles, whelks, plankton drifting
into bloom, halibut, coho, chum, the small gray tail
slipping from the belly slit, screaming cliffs
of kittiwakes, tide marshes filled with snipe,
cranes, grebes, scaup, duck, forty-pound swans,
even the eagle sitting in the dead spruce, waiting
for the red and silver rivers to flow upstream.

# JOHN MUIR REMEMBERS ELIZA HENDRICKS

Eliza, if
wood smoke had not hung above the road
if the road had not been warmed, then cooled, then warmed
then frozen over with ice too smooth
to give firm footing
if we had not seen the ruffed grouse perched
in the poplar like a fat, mottled pear
if its flanks had not been puffed
or streaked with brown
its tail not fanned with silver
if it had not been feeding on winter buds
if it had not been silent
if it had drummed or whirred its wings
or lifted its ruff or called
if it had been afraid of you
or me, if you had not pressed your hand gently
against the small of my back, if the grouse
had not smoothed its feathers
not arched its neck
not raised its crest
not lengthened its body slowly
opening like a fist unclenching
if you had not touched me
if the bird had not tilted its head
to listen to us breathe
if there had been a wind
if the bird had separated itself from the tree
to fly down close
to the ground with rapid wingbeats sweeping away the invisible

intricate paths of mice
if the sun had not burned through the smoke
or parted the haze or surrounded
your hair with light
then I would have walked back with you that afternoon
to the house where the pewter bowls sat
on the oak table in the room where I used to watch you
ironing sheets, opening each crumpled hem, smoothing
the lace with cast iron and steam, I would
not have to bear the weight of all
the wings I've failed to see,
all of them folded in the tops
of the closest trees, Eliza,
I wish I had not fled from you.

# KANTISHNA MORNING


Iridescent green
darners fly by, joined midair,
together upside

down and rightside up—
one quick glimpse of the water through
their wings, wavering.

They skim
the river's shadows, turning
tusk-white in the sun.

## YOU SAY YOU LOVE HOW
## UNEXPECTED, OPEN FIELDS

balance themselves on mountain sides,
    how shadows smooth the snow at dusk
        until the ice ribbing the cabin path

is impossible to see.
    You say "Look. Across the slough—the forest's burning."
        My face goes slack, I see

the flames and then I see
    the man feeding armfuls of cut brush to a yard fire.
        You say when you were eight

your favorite horse turned its back on you
    and kicked your legs until you could not
        move. Your father carried you inside.

It took you weeks to learn to walk
    with the hoof branded on your hip, turning
        black. Now you say you love

the way night makes the forest seem small
    and how at night I fool myself into thinking
        no trees grow past the reach of our cabin lights.

You say "The car won't start"
    when it is twenty below.
        Then you turn the keys. Love,

you are teaching me. I am learning
        to keep my eyes open
                even in my dreams. Tonight we drive

along the river road. You gasp and jerk your hands
        as if the steering wheel burns your skin,
                poising your hands above the wheel

in the air as the car drifts towards the ledge.
        A thread of water weaves itself
                through the canyon. Horses walk

by the river, dark specks against the sandstone.
        Close to the ledge
                I lift one hand, as if to wave

to someone standing in the air in front of us. You grab
        the wheel and ease the car towards the asphalt
                but I'm already falling. I am falling

slowly, trying to swim back up. Soon I will be standing
        on a ridge of rock
                watching you run towards me

past the slope where the spruce replace the birch. New snow
        will fall all around us, chiming against my coat, against
                itself, against

the hard, white ground.
    I'll see a horse running up the stream bed and your eyes
        will have the translucence of fingers

pressed together and held up against the sun.

# BODHISATTVA

He just sits there, half-kneeling, big-bellied.
If only I could turn or walk away
from those gesso-shadowed eyes holding me

benched on the third floor of this museum
while Somalis scratch for grain in hard clay.
He just sits there, half-kneeling, big-bellied.

Men tear down their hand-built homes in Haiti
and burn the wood to feed their children for a day.
Green, gesso-shadowed eyes are holding me.

In Pernambuco, Brazilian mothers cannot grieve
another baby's death. Most children die unnamed.
He just sits there, half-kneeling, big-bellied.

Gunblasts open all the windows permanently—
now wind and snow rip into Sarajevo.
Gesso-shadowed eyes are holding me

headphoned to the news, focused on other cities seized,
well-fed, rich enough to own a radio.
He just sits there, half-kneeling, big-bellied,

while I try to forget how I failed to catch Lizzie
falling this morning face-first on the pavement.
He just sits there, half-kneeling, big-bellied,
his green, gesso-shadowed eyes holding me.

# NEAR NENANA

All around us water churns.
We're stuck inside a
pool that's stuck inside itself.
        Current-tipped, the boat
lurches like a horse gone bad,
        trying to get rid of us.
        The whirling water turns and
turns, circling around
        the hole where everything goes
                down, the funnel wide
        enough and poised to take us
                down. Try the throttle?
I follow your eyes following
        the line we've got to
                follow to get out. Who could
swim this pool? I've seen
        maps of underwater cliffs
                arroyoed and cleft, sheer-
dropped despite the water's clutch
        rounding every ridge,
                pulled through silt, stone conduit-drawn
to chambers I can't
        see. The motor guns, slips us
                sideways, slant-tacked. Some-
where, talons sink into soft
        bark. You cut the fuel,
                lift the prop, stop the motor.
Steel blades cut the air,
        pause. Somewhere dark birds rest some-
                how in the sea, bills
tipped to the sky, wings held out

wind-ruffed and sun-dried,
          waiting. Have you given up? Some-
where a cliffed horse
          scrambles in loose rock. We have
               so much planned! You just sit
there while the boat sways, our knees
          press the chine, then we're
               moving, the boat is slowly
moving, easing through,
          like a horse let be, allowed
               to find her own path
across the sliding shale slope.

# TOLOVANA

Moths gather on the bark
slowly raising and lowering their wings
in the heat

of the burning tree
mowed down last spring by the ice breaking up

on this sandbar gradually sloping

we sit back to back
shoulder blades pressed together
bones and ligaments aching
as if we had wings
wrapped
in too many layers of cloth

a moth hovers close
you hold her with your eyes
the way I once saw a Yup'ik hunter hold a feather

poised above the ice hole
to receive the breath of the seal
he knew would exhale
just before she came up for air

thick ice, winter water

she never saw
the ivory-tipped spear in line with her chest

your hand snatches the air
the moth disappears into the darkness
of your fist

in less time
than it takes to disturb the wing scales so easily broken
you turn your hand over

and finger by finger, slowly open your grasp

she pauses for a moment
then takes off

# THE BREEZE NUDGES THE JUNIPERS, PROMISING

cool air soon. Forget the talk of Grandpa's
tests, doctor this and doctor that, grown-ups
casting glances at the *Atlas of the Human Body*

left open on the kitchen counter all day, road
maps networked in red and blue around a place
none of us knew, broken pumps, melted casings,

forty acres left so dry the cattle lay down
motionless. Birds panting. Remember the dust
devils dancing in the driveway? Their swirling

made you laugh. Now you cry for Daddy's-Daddy
as if he's gone somewhere. The branches outside
our window move between us and the moon

pulling us together in a waving,
underwater web of shadow and light, rocking
both of us towards the man whose heart

ticks at the center of this house. Grandpa's
okay now, sleeping in the room
next to ours. If you close your eyes you might

see the jagged mountains we flew above to get
here, new green softening the edges of the ash
slopes rimmed with trees laid down in rows,

polished silver by the heat. Drift down, sleep-
winged cottonwood seed, count miles of open ditches
carrying the Deschutes to pastures filled

with sage, green rabbit bush, fescue, thistle,
bitter brush, manzanita, and wild rose. The pig
bends her legs and slowly sinks into her wallow.

The gray-mantled ground squirrel burrows deep,
curling close to cool roots. The chickens cluck
around brimming pails. Slow-eyed horses lower

their muzzles into troughs and the grownups stop
pacing the living room as if it were an airport.
In your sleep, see us fill our glasses with

clear water pulled from lava rock six hundred
feet below, talking lazily of water rights, as if
tonight were any night, all of us together.

# DEAR HIPPOPOTAMUS

Move over, you tiny-eared, boulder-bodied
hog, let me kneel down with you, bleary-eyed
and mud-sunk. Water horse! Let me wallow
in your ivory-stained, peg-toothed dreams, following
the cool, sun-chased shadows while flamingos
arrive screeching pink from their distant coasts.
News of shocking continents! Let's listen
to the twirling, sliding, feathered whistles
of their courting colors, blurred and whirlpooled
down still air, like the bristling pods of burr seeds,
or the spinning of the wasp-stung beetle,
or the circling of the zinc-lined stars, reeling
night after night above your small, revolving
ears, while our great, slow, rock-bound bodies sleep.

## WHERE THE LONG, LAZY
## MOTHERS STROLL

with their children running ahead, the shore
is as messy as any other grassy edge
where birds nest, rock spotted,
blotched by gulls, geese, and gadwalls.

Into the flocks, unexpected
outburst of a hundred startled teal,
wingtips all together, thrumming the air
this close! Almost to touch. Wet sand

slopped by my daughter's small hands fast enough
to streak pastel corduroy dark dun.
Into the roll of waves yanked out
to sea by the eggshell china saucer

moon rising in full day. Into the rasp
of branches blurred by shawls of falling
petals. Into the barely perceptible lapping
of the feral cat drinking muddy water

from the run-off ditch, in that moment
just before dusk when everything
quiets—my daughter
seems small, still in sight—I could race to her—

I could yell—at this moment—
mine is the sloth of the hawk
steady in the cottonwood while crows drive
their beaks through the air as close

to my eyes as the wind. Mine is the torpor
of old travelers who have seen shores like this
in Nantes, Rio, Zanzibar, New York. Mine
is the languor of the young who believe even

the eldest can always go back home. Mine
is the lethargy of faith. I remember following
my own mother's journeys on my grandmother's
pre-war porcelain globe that glowed slightly yellow

with the light of its old, twenty-watt bulb shining
through the countries, still brightly colored,
red, yellow, green. Can you believe it? After
all these years. I remember reaching up to touch

the glass sphere high on the shelf, following my
mother's flights one day, boats the next, tracing my
mother with my hands as if I were blind,
as if I were still a child, studying my mother's

face with my fingertips, and my mother, without
being asked, stood still for a moment, just for a moment.

# DREAM OF THE HAWK

*1.*

Just to see the clouds clearly and the true
gray of unbroken sky! Some will do anything.
The windows ring. Something's wrong
with the sky. The birds see
unexpected doors, blue-gray and white, wide open—
even with the curtains pulled
they keep hurling themselves into what they see
as sky. Towards me. I feel those welcome,
blowzy feet flutter on my ribs
and then the rake of endless furrows stretching
after they have gone. Gone! Unannounced.
Our next-door neighbor, Aina, picks them up
and gently sets them under the juniper hedge.
Who's strong enough to care? All these broken
sparrows, voles, rabbits, field mice. Even the hawk needs
food. Where can I go where I won't hear
the sound of feathers hitting glass?
Where is my wide-winged one now?

2.

who hovers over the field
suspending herself just above the ground
rising as the clumps of grass rise
falling as the gullies fall
tracking the contours of the old hay mounds under the snow
her gray wings tipped with charcoal as if passed
through flame
her gaze unbroken, bill turned down
cream-colored neck and belly scalloped
deep sienna, barely visible, feather-stenciled
swirls of lace. She lowers her legs, opens her claws
and pounces.
Grasps grass.
Still-open wings, already airborne—
tufts of feathers on her upper legs billowing—
she grabs more dirt. Again. Snow. Again. Gravel.
Striking, rising, landing, clutching nothing
hovering, empty clawed

3.

who says unborn children drift above the mountains waiting

who strokes her powerful wings over the lakes
to find the geese balanced close to each other,
one-legged. They know corn will come, strewn
by men carrying burlap bags. Even in the snow.
They're sure. I don't know. I hope
though it's late
and there's just
the hawk hunched over on a drift, the wind
lifting her feathers, mud-colored, white
in places, like the snow, and the light
is silver reflected off the bright,
full corners of the field, which by now
should be dark, just turning to green

*4.*

who watches the crow as he dives beak-first to catch
whatever. He's got it. Now he's dropped it
and it falls in a free-twirling spiral
and he plunges, twisting like a maple seed,
breaking out of his cone-shaped plummet
to snatch it from the air
and let it drop—again—as if this were a game—
this holding and releasing

*5.*

who clamps something
soft and feathered, like a fancy gray purse the size of an orange
but not an orange
on the branch between her claws
and the bark. She holds tight. She knows
what the wind wants.

Tilting her head, she studies the sky,
flicks her tail, bends back down to work
and without meaning to begins to reveal
its true hollowness, this open space, this handful

of air marked by slender, curved bones
bent like the struts of a small, wicker
cricket cage. She plucks carefully, releasing
downy tufts into the wind, and the wind
lifts each feather over the rough rail fence

as she pulls the long, silver threads from the places
where they once laced everything together.
It resists. With a sort of stiffness,

the struts refuse to give up their arc
even as she unbends them one by one
with her beak. They snap back, saying
You've taken enough. No more.
Her charcoal cap feathers spread out

over her back like a cape. From her mottled
upper thighs emerge long legs, shockingly yellow.
Her tail is white, barred with rust, chestnut on top
darker underneath
and when she fans it open

the feathers split, as if she has two tails.
She is missing many feathers. Late spring
and the snow is still deep. The mockingbirds, jays,
pigeons, and crows have disappeared. Her eyes
are gold and constantly searching

6.

who sees the shadows shifting from stem to branch to trunk
alert with squirrel, shrew, cardinal, moth
and I feel hunger like the wind
uncontained by open fields
full-footed now
and quick enough to slice tendons
apart for someone I have never met
as I sleep on my side, dreaming of enameled
stoves, avocados out of season
and a patch of dirt thousands of miles east
inhabited by hummingbirds and crabgrass
and the wind
fingers the hollows of my bones
giving flight to beach stones, blue talus slopes,
shale bluffs, snow-crowded skies,
exquisite gifts, the sight of which
turns the wind away
and in this lightness, I hold her
close within every
cloud-stained, feather-colored cliff uplifting.

## DEPARTURE

Thousands of tiny
fists tamp the surface of the lake
flowing like a wide
river gone crazy, southeast, westnorth
letting the wind push
it around in its bed. The boat
hull hugs the shore.
What else can she do? Even the trees
agree, shaking
their crowns, throwing down their leaves as if
she were their only
child. Caught cold-footed in Magnuson
grass, trying to cut
free of the creosote-soaked pilings sunk
deep in the shallow
mud holding the water, holding her
wake for a moment,
furrow folding back over into
confusion. Cascade
gray cross-currents! Sharp switching eddies!
Unreliable
shoals! Let the cloth argue with itself,
gasping like a child
with the air knocked out and the wind
socking the center.
Let the sail, shot-silk green and white, now
snapping, billowing
slowly draw her away from this beach
lined with broken glass, rocks
as smooth as plovers' eggs, and small
stones splashed iron red

and orange like the sky breaking open.
Let the windows ignite
flickering copper on the other shore.
Let the water be
disked with silver from here to there
churning as if roiled
by the flanks of a great, gentle fish.

# II

# THE ROAD TO
# MARSHFIELD LAKE

# THE ROAD TO MARSHFIELD LAKE

*1.*

The chimebird teeters on the table's edge,
starts to fall, rocks back and forth, beak-
first, somehow comes to stand again.

With your hands to steady hers, she grabs
the Matreshka doll, pulls apart the halves,
lifts out the smaller figure, then the next,
each pear-shaped belly hinged to hold one more
red, blue, green, yellow, hand-painted, smocked, and smiling
face until the smallest

rests inside your palm. She laughs, trilling
like a bicycle bell, our daughter, one year old
but as tipsy and loose-jointed as Raggedy Ann.

2.

Splendid in his white coat and confidence, the doctor

3.

This is the concrete cathedral
   nestled in hills close to the river
      we drove for hours to find.
These are the big, gray blocks
   stacked on top of each other, honeycombed
      with hundreds of glass rooms
         just like the one we wait in now.
That is the asphalt, far below
   and those are the plows crumpling the snow
      as soft as fine, white flannel
         heaped into drifts speckled with gravel.
Those are the doctors and nurses
   rushing from door to door
      in the courtyard four stories below
         on thread-thin trails
            trampled by tiny feet
We drove for hours to find.

4.

The doctor returns, bringing more doctors.
A voice from the wall calls them away.

5.

The land outside has gone wild, corn
and timothy abandoned,
snow-filled fields stitched with lines of gulls
all along the lake. The late spring
snow has covered all the aster, goldenrod, and phlox seeds.
In the shadows, two people walk along the shore,
pulling a sled. A dog lopes
in wide circles around them, chasing skiffs of snow,
returning to greet the man and the woman again and again.
The orange-berried branches piled in the sled
shift, and a child emerges. Clambering out, she waves
her arms. They wait for her to catch up.
She's just a little girl, running
on her own two legs. The gulls, startled, rise up,
one flock, then scattered wings, then one again.

6.

She sleeps sitting in my lap, her face pressed
between my breasts, wrapped in a crib sheet
crowded with dancing elephants.
When I close my eyes I see a juniper branch
suspended in the ice below my feet.
Far below me, in the lake
barely visible
in a room of water,
tangled in the long green stems of water grass
swaying in the silt
beneath the three-foot ceiling of ice
hardening between the lake bed and the sky—
a child stands.

7.

The eye, the doctor says, is a door
    that opens willingly to a perfect
corridor of light, the optic nerve, wide
    enough to lead a penlight's beam into
the soft gray folds inside the skull.

8.

In your eyes, I see the night you and I
lay together on the blue and green sheets
whose corners came undone while strips of white
tulle fluttered just above our bed,
your arms around me until it seemed
polished cotton pastels hung, ceiling secured, in pleats,
and broadloom carpeted the walls.
Our old mattress wrapped in down-filled doeskin,
each pillow encased with mohair ticking. Linen
cambric and challis floated in and out the window,
white gossamer drifted in the air, draped
all around us, bolts of uncut jersey, bright
stripes and beige, and with each movement
of our bodies touching, unfolding lengths
laid themselves down on top of us, brocade,
worsted, chenille, limbs curving around
each other, yards of gingham, felt, batiste,
supportive, not restricting, resilient
billows of lamé, handfuls of chambray filling the room.

9.

Two hundred eighty days and more we waited—
remember how you caught her?
Just as she tore through the rough tide's breaking waves,
capped with soft, brown hair. Cow-licked and lambent,
she flailed her bright pink arms and legs.
You held her on my chest and wrapped her
in white flannel. Folded then, inside
my arms, she opened her deep-water blue eyes
and gathered us together in her gaze.

*10.*

In her eyes, I see the soft blue of familiar
mountains and beyond—polished granite
outcrops and teal shadows shading
rosebay, sandwort, and labrador tea.
Snow piles on the ledge of rock
sloping to the valley from black spruce and balsam fir
to beech and birch. The stone funnels the wind.
Cracked with cold comes the fissure she falls
down. Down the slick, slate roof under which
she cries until her parents swaddle her
in flannel tight enough to make her safe inside the room
too wide for her to see across and filled with corners,
unforgiving hardwood floors, ruled by gravity,
unannounced, pulls her down, sideways, down
to greet her flesh, while her parents
hover close by, well-intentioned, powerless.

*11.*

Everything I want to know is blurred
into an endless "will-she, will-she, will-she," murmured
as if by a marsh bird standing, watching
the late spring snow slowly fall around her clutch.

*12.*

The doctor turns away and weeps.

13.

Down blown clouds, coming fast. It seems
someone high above is sledging cement walls
apart, then sweeping up what's left, swirling
scree, rubble, dust, and brash. As fast as they
are swept away—a new batch breaks overhead.

*14.*

The nurse walks in, wants to take
her for just two minutes, for
a photograph. She lifts her,
warm and sleepy, from my arms—

*15.*

The eighth-floor corridor
is banked with windows. Where
have they taken her? I see
fragments of the land outside
broken by the new highway
and the old road, far below
separated from itself
like pieces of a river
oxbowed into lakes, unwanted
asphalt bulldozed,
tons of spall, cement bullocks,
house-sized heaps of sand,
streams of cars
crawling on a single, unpaved lane, hundreds
of gravel-struck windshields casting
the sunlight
away in all directions.

*16.*

The child tries to lift her head, to grab one
of the crib's railing rungs, to pull herself
up, half-sitting, slipping grasp, falling back
protesting, red-faced, clench-fisted, kicking mad.

*17.*

Give my daughter back to me.

*18.*

Now I see the road home, south
past Blodgett Brook, Whaleback Ridge, Sunapee,
Bela Pond, Weare, and far out on Marshfield Lake, a family
walking over cattail and dry grass-stippled ice.

The woman carries blankets and clothes, the man holds
his coat closed against the wind cutting
through the corduroy, billowing in the space
where their daughter sleeps, wrapped in down and wool,

snug in the canvas pouch, both hands resting
on her father's collarbones. The wind is streaked
with sleet. The pockmarked
ice holds them up, ribbed here like poplin,

there, clear amber silk. We are walking
towards the cluster of small houses
set on the ice above the shallows, close
to the point where the fog-shawled pines are tipped deep jade.
A leaf rasps across the ice. Electric
lines whine. A station wagon's tailgate
slams, and then voices, not so far away.

*19.*

Other families, unloading near the bobhouses.
Men, women, and children dressed in cotton-batted, zippered
suits and quilted snowmobile boots, pulling
sleds filled with children, crowbars, augers, reels
of 15-pound line, tip-ups, tarps, Carlisles, and sheathed knives,
out on the ice, unfolding chairs
around the burning driftwood. The wind brings
scraps of what might be there, wood smoke and talk of jigging lines,
barometers, kerosene cookers, coffee,
stew, coolers to keep the food from freezing,

20.

and children trading handfuls of sparsely-tied,
cut-winged, wet flies for tobacco tins of bait, children turning
to wave at us as we approach, riding
on their fathers' shoulders, children pointing
and laughing at the crowd of thermoses set askew
in snow. Men and women throw quick smiles
over their shoulders, greeting us with brief
waves as they work. We see people who might know

what comes next,
the anchoring of aluminum poles and canvas
to make a windstop,
the sitting quietly for hours,
tying and untying knots
inside a little house with no windows,
just aqua light filtering through
transparent floors,
light reflected from the bottom of the ice.

# III

# STORM

# TONGA RIDGE

Sitting on the slope
scattered with ponchos, diapers, spare socks,
and the caterpillar-brown army blanket

the quiet inhalations of Elizabeth's sleep
blending with the bustle of leaves and plastic bags,
her father and grandmother talking
softly, picking berries

the swish of my hand
sweeping the mosquitoes from her face,
the flies and the bees muttering,

and far beyond the dark green forests
slashed with the silver dead,
something drones like a slow-moving Cessna,
though there are no planes in sight.

For a moment I see
beyond the snow patches and the distant
jagged ridges
veined with gravel run-offs too steep to hold trees

how many times this trail has been traveled
by one family or another,
led by the eldest woman

who knows the way up the Foss River road
to the trail head,
one woman leading one small group single file
into the pale green pines,

through the long-bristled branches draped
with moss, and the new platinum-gray needles billowing

along the ridge
where layers of warm air trapped
by the high, flamboyant storm clouds
are streaked with cool breezes

and into the thistle-gone-to-seed meadows
and the fireweed hung with mauve stork-bill pods,

to a spot where a mother might rest
with her child sleeping at her side,
on the blanket pressing the wild grass
close in with the blueberries' maroon-edged leaves
and the triangular handshakes of ferns.

## JOHN MUIR DREAMS

The firs, the aspens, all the other trees
stand up straight, but the snow
holds one birch down so far its crown

is buried in a drift. I ski
knee-deep to reach it and I beat
the snow with my hardwood pole,

thrusting the basket deep to break
the mound. The tree heaves, rises
about a foot, and hangs there, bobbing

up and down. I grab one branch
and yank it hard. One mound splits,
falls so fast it hits my face—no time

to jump away. I trip, lose my feet,
cling to the branch. I feel the wood's memory,
the tension in its grain. Then the branch

falls. I taste the snow. The snow
accepts my hands, my arms, my legs.
I struggle to stand up but there's nothing

to push against. The surface of the snow
is as rough as steel wool. The field
turns pale yellow, the trees streak

the field with slate. The sun forces
itself around the edges of the far hills.
I feel the weight of the dark hills, the weight

of the light on my legs. I lie there
with my arms stretched out and my hands open
and the light pools in my palms.

## DUSK CHOIR

We slipped under the split-rail fence,
Maggie and I. Our bodies left wings in the snow.
The new powder rose up around our feet
and we ran to get away from Father.
Stopped at George Duncan's. Twenty-four dogs
chained up in his front yard. Howling, filling
our ears with sound. They were pure
sound. Their mouths. Feet. Legs. Their bones.
The clink of tin buckets. George Duncan ladled
ground horse meat and corn meal, slopping one ladle
on each pine slab, one ladle for each dog
except the one who had not pulled the sled hard
enough. He said she was not worth the cost
of corn. Then they were quiet, lapping.
We could smell the cereal and blood.
The one dog shook as she watched
the others eat. We listened to the lapping,
wet tongues on wood. Beyond the trees, Fountain Lake
moved against the shore, blue and cold, its ice skin
split by straps of light. If we crawled under
the lake ice, Maggie and I, the water would fill
our ears. Pure water. When we crawled out
we'd stand on top of the ridge
with the hickories and burr oaks looking
east at Father's barns. Our farmhouse would look
small, smaller than a doghouse. The dog looked
at us. She had one blue eye and one gold eye.

# SEPARATION

This is the world
round and wet
rafted with dirt
peopled with parents

whose daughter closes her eyes in the bathtub
feeling the water abandon her legs
as it leaks down the drain
in the house whose big windows face south

sucking in sunlight
expanding the rooms
where her father cared for the plants
when he lived here, touching the dirt

to see what they needed, the roots of the aloe
suspended in baskets of hand-knotted twine
crowding the panes, pots heavy with water
stems curved by the weight of the leaves

chewed by the cat who slept on the shelf
swayed by books next to the mugs
stained with coffee, cracked by the stove
loaded with slabwood from the forest out back

crammed with trees that scratch the sky
bloated with snow
seen by the girl who sits in the tub
naming each thing in the house

to make things stay
while she waits for her mother to take her
to the bed swollen with pillows

as white as the claw-footed, sparkling, stainless, white,
polished, porcelain
tub that does not

hold water, the bathtub that holds nothing.

# ANIMALS, DISAPPEARING

I keep coming back to these steep,
sloped hills of sphagnum moss,
waiting for you to uncurl from
your nests, shake the snow off

your thick furs, bodies as white as
the winter sky, arms
and legs as dark as wet bark.
If only you would rise,

alive again. There's so much
I don't understand. You
raked the side of the closest spruce,
sat down under the tree,

pulled in your long, curved claws, and stroked
the infants tucked against
your chests. Boulder-bellied mothers!
I once called you *metal*

*eaters*, said you ate copper
and iron in the Sapphire
Mountains north of Skalkaho. This
was not true! In the shade

of the hollow fir where you gave
birth to all of us, I
lay covered with needles, maple
leaves, the smell of quince.

Bamboo flowered in the valley.
I slept, dreaming of
white fog floating down so thick
it seemed as if nothing

beyond the den existed. Surrounded
by pheasant, viburnum,
woodpeckers, takin, and your bodies'
deep musk always close by

we moved together
in stands of bentgrass stretching for miles.
Many things frighten me—
birch trees heavy with frost,

frozen hemlock needles, coat-soaking
snow. How quickly the rhododendron,
tufted sedge, pikas, deer, rocks, streams,
and distant white mountains

dissolved. How carefully
I watched you holding the infants
gently in your broad limbs, tipping
them onto the ground filled

with breath, bones, spit, blood, and milk.
How I still need
to hear your hearts drumming within
the skin of this world.

# THE WILD DOG'S STEPS

Envy the wild dog stalking on the snow's
   wavering path and his ice-imprinted steps.
      The water snake disappears. Her rope-looped
wake takes longer to erase, diminishing
   in ever-widening arcs. Falling always
      down, the rain is pulled towards the earth's iron
heart. A pair of hawks press their bellies, turn hooked heads,
   entangle talons, free-fall towards slate
      roofs. Sprung at the seam, each barely touching,
the Scot's broom's pods burst open, twisting old
   husks in two. Swooping north over the slope
      in broad day, the short-eared owl embraces
the hill beyond the chain-link fence with the wide


      ovals of her flight. Hooped wings direct the air.
      Dark lines ellipse shoulders, face. Overhead,
the geese hurl their collective weight along
   triangulated necks. Does the milkweed
      doubt the wind? Held out like children's hands,
the hawthorne's leaves cup themselves,
   fastened to green limbs shooting up and down
      in a rush of yellow-red as bent as
water falling from a spring no one can
   see. A pheasant whirs her blustered feathers
      upwards. Another nests his ring-marked chest
in sable grass, parting wide with wasps. Yet
   somehow each is whole. Dear pale, displaced feet,
      abandoned! Envy them.

# THE TIDE, THE MOON

She'd like to run down the beach
with the other kids but he wants her,
wants to give her the rock hammer.
He keeps the ice pick, keeps her close

to him. He's teaching her about the tide,
the moon, the wine-red stones. He tells her
"In half an hour the waves will rise. In two
they'll touch your feet, in three your knees,

in four your thighs." He touches her to show
where the waves will touch. "In five
the rock you sit on will be gone." She turns
away, searches hard for garnets in the mica

schist. He's old enough to be her grandfather.
"The moon weighs more than the sea.
That's what makes the tides move." She taps
a small stone loose and sees endless arms,

spiked beads of light rolling inside. "In
Norway someone found a garnet boulder—1500
pounds." She thinks of disappearing stones—
heavy, white, soft. Easily cleaved. Invisible

in water. They weigh enough to anchor boats.
He stares at her and chews his gum. Around,
around, around his mouth moves. He pulls her
by the arm behind the sand hill to show her

a patch of andradite on the wall. "It's nice,
you'll see." There are no garnets. He pulls
her down. "I want to show you something."
She hears the kids at the far end of the beach,

they don't hear her. She fights. She learns why
the sea obeys a body bigger than itself, betrays
things smaller than itself, why limestone touched
with vinegar hisses, why it leaves white streaks.

Quiet. No one knows why she's so quiet. She listens
to him tell the class about mud under the sea,
how water presses down on it until it turns to shale,
listens to him teach how to turn garnets in the tumbling

machine, how to smooth rough gems with silicon
grit and water, how to polish stones with diamond
grit and olive oil, how to keep the grit from
grinding the stones into fistfuls of rose-colored dust.

# DRIFTWOOD

Barely buoyant, sea-hollowed, salt-

smoothed, tempted by the shore's dun rocks

and sand, cold, iron clouds arcing

over, waterlogged, curled

wind moving inside the center

knot, slowly unwinding. Sinking,

wave-rocked, lingering, soft and hard

wood scraping wood, water churning

patience, the only sanctity

as trunks strive for symmetry, small

limbs bend, winged stumps

holding up against the slate shelves

of the sky, the lure of a blue-streaked

desire to crumble in the wet,

be beached, dried out, pulled open at

the seams. Sooty, gravel-bound, floating

close enough to touch, each one held

as if by folds of sudden rain

embracing stem, sea, air, sand, and

you and me, curtains slowly opening

in the shallows where the sodden,

no longer listless, yearn to see

what current moves within the core

now pliant, irresistibly, also

drifting, bearing light.

## WHY I DID IT

Things nobody
sees
happen in North Dakota.

I looked down in the gully
and there was all of Medina
laid out in the gulch.
The only moving things were the hawks
and me.
Trucks, sometimes.
After that it got flatter—

nothing but fields of sunflowers,
stems bent,
almost touching the ground.
Sometimes, when I didn't know how fast
I was driving,
I'd look up and see a hawk sitting
on a fence post,
his belly white in the sun,
facing the wind with his chest,
like a masthead
on a boat I couldn't see.

No winter wheat,
no mallard, no blue herons,
just the range cut up with barbwire.
I couldn't stand it in the car anymore.
There was nowhere else to go.
I looked up—
a rough-legged hawk hovered

above the fences,
his body a dark silhouette
edged with silver light.

The air glowed.

My husband said
if you see a red-tailed hawk
coming at you at dusk,
flying low,
you'll see the light-colored wrist marks
on his wings
as a pair of headlights.

There's a difference between them,
my husband taught me.
The long-tailed hawk
bucks the wind with his shoulders,
cuts a path head-on

for the rest of his body to follow,
then dives straight down on his prey.
The fan-tailed hawk hovers
on top of the wind,
cups his wings
over the ledge where the air meets the sky,
then dives down on his prey.

Birds always
seem to get away.
They dip close to your windshield,

their feathers almost touch the metal,
then some invisible string
yanks them away.

Once, right after we were married,
I saw a young hawk's eyes.
He spiraled down, his body carving
a helix in the air.
Just before he touched the ground,
he caught himself
and looped back up again,
belly up,
he glanced at us before he turned his head away.
How bright his eyes were.

I drove for no reason.
Just to drive.
I don't know why I left him,
why I threw our set of 1930s glassware
in boxes in the back seat.
I kept thinking
I've got to have something to eat on.

Near Belfield the wind got bad.
It began to rain.
I passed one
hunched over on an irrigation pipe,
his feathers all roughed up,
like he was pretending to be a gargoyle.
There wasn't enough rain to settle the dust.
The wipers rasped against the glass,

making the sound
stone makes
against metal.

Sometimes my husband
would sit all afternoon,
sharpening his axe,
grinding the rough edge smooth
with short, then long
strokes.

I could not tell him
how frightened I was.
I kept thinking—
I've just got to
wait until it gets better.

The wet culverts made me keep thinking
of the storms back home,
how the rain gathers on the hills where the trees
were cut,
carrying the sandy loam downhill,
washing out
the loose-rooted grass,
carrying everything green
downhill, leaving dirt
ditches everywhere.

*Sharp-shinned, Ferruginous, Rough-legged,*
*Broad-winged, Red-shouldered,*

my husband knew them all.
He'd call out a name
after seeing just a shadow,
he was always right.

Once, when I refused to carry in the groceries,
he taught me he was right
with his hands.

I didn't see it coming,
no headlights, no sound,
nothing,

it was just there,
drifting towards my lane,
floating
towards my car, huge,
he came towards me.
I saw his rust-colored shoulders.
My hands

locked. I didn't
swerve, I didn't
think, I
just kept driving.

## STEHEKIN LIGHT

As if skimming bare-skinned on this fifty
mile glacial trough filled with liquid
ice, the girls in wet suits fly by, waving—

tied to their speed boats, they dig
their heels in and ride in circles
around our tourist barge. Just lean

back, lock your knees! their bodies grin.
The lake feeds on delft-blue
springs which seep from rockbed cracks.

Trout sleep in the silt. The common
loon moves through easy currents. Along
the shore, flame-colored moths falter,

fall open-winged, plaster themselves
on shallow pools. The yellow jackets
move in. Swing down, pick up the moths

and carry them, dangling, all the way
to mud nests clenched like hidden fists
in the scrub, high on the talus slopes

that hold this lake in place. The girls
turn graceful flips on the waves, spinning
spiral somersaults, falling, rising,

walking on the lake. The water
is as black as crankcase oil. The sun
pours ropes of molten brass around

the girls as it sinks low, tangles
their feet in silver cords, copper wires,
and braided strands of spun-glass light,

tightening the knot as it goes down.

# JOHN MUIR'S HICKORY CLOCK

I took it down to the root cellar,
took it all apart, held its pieces
in my hands. To study them, to copy
them. I knew they were not mine.
I heard Mother cry. She hid her face
from Father but he saw and made her
tell him what was wrong. He beat
Maggie until she could not cry. I hid
downstairs and Maggie never told him. Maggie,
Mother held you after he was done, ladled
water, sponged the cuts with tea, poulticed
your back. Nothing helped. The next day I built
the scythe-shaped clock. When Father left
to preach, we sat next to Mother,
next to the stove. *You can tell when the fire*
*gets too big,* she said, *it turns the metal*
*orange. See? Its heart is white, its hands*
*are red.* She told us about the boy who looked
straight up at the sun's eclipse. *Never look*
*at fires in the sky.* Now all I see
are dusty window panes. Outside, the sun
turns white, the sky turns white, the sun
tries to burn its way out. Even with my
eyes closed—ragged light, unexpected
countersuns, swirling, encircling compasses,
waterwheels, windmills, cogwheels,
rakes, bradawls, joinings, thermometers,
pyrometers, door locks, clocks, this light
embracing everything I've ever tried to fix.

# SLOWLY, TURNING EACH EDGE UNDER

Stumbling, your fingers learned to fold the cloth
slowly, turning each edge under to make a point
sixteen times for every square, none of which could fray
or else you'd be to blame, again the scapegrace
of La Grange county. Piles of blocks and border strips
lined up on the workroom table, waiting to be pieced

into bigger squares. Layers of worsted sat half-pieced
with quills, half-cinched with sleep's teeth. The cloth
was as dark as the shadows in a new-moon sky stripped
of street lamps. You wanted to stitch all those star points
up where they belonged, tack together that landscape
come undone. Heaps of mustard flowers cut from frayed

meadows lay in your lap. How easily the fabric frayed!
Not long before, the elders' gentle, peaceful
glances had praised your handwork. You said you felt His grace
move through your fingertips, covering new cloth
with coral, purl, daisy, rose, shell, point,
and satin stitches curved to border blocks of the striped

sampler spelling *thank you.* From your stripped
heart to the Hochstetlers, who had taken you, frayed
and parentless, into their home years before, and pointed
out the sun-slashed fields all around the house, pieced
and planted by the living. You worked that dark cloth
with light. But when the deacon came, he saw—not God's grace—

no, he said he saw the devil's ornate arguments, a hellscape
twisted through the thread you held. You stripped
the cambric clean. Gathered yards of kettle cloth,

praying twelve straight stitches might help unfray
one inch of damage done. Sometimes, when I see pieces
of threadbare fog floating just above the pointed

pines like a sail set loose, then torn by the pointed
branches and roofs it wraps itself around, gracefully,
like bolts of old challis ripping into endless pieces,
the early morning mist hovers near the ground in strips,
and I think of how you might have waited for the sun's frayed
fist to open, to reach down from the sky and touch the cloth,

to turn your neighbors towards the point on the striped horizon
where the land's edge, frayed and ripped, is mended,
bright shreds of sheared cloth woven whole in darkness.

## PALE STONES

It's hard to believe

this beach
rests on plates of rock that shift

constantly.

We crawl
along the shore with the birds,
sifting

the gravel for bright blue agates.
You say we must
find them before spring, before the summer waves.
All morning we talked

about whether to stay
together.

We throw the pale stones away.
The sandpipers lift
together, like a single,
singed scarf
caught by the wind.

You say the earth
is a soft-centered fruit
whose core is warm—
I thrust my hands wrist-deep
in the dark, wet sand.
I fear the earth is a skull

made of pieces
that barely touch.
We throw a few

more stones away.

Caught between us
and the waves,
the dowitcher scurries
away. She takes off—
I hear her single,

sharp *keeeeeep.*

# SHORTHORNS

Heavy-hocked, barrel-bellied,
exhaling billows of steam, they wait
while the corn, wheat, clover,
and potato fields surround us, finished
for the season. We listened to their hooves
shift. Blue tongues lick black shoulders,
impatient horns stab the ground.
Soon Father will open the gate
to where to the last crop sits
sun-softened, stem ends dark, sinking

back into the dirt. For pulling plows,
for yanking oak and hickory grubs
up by the roots, for heaving stumps,
for stopping one night on the way home
from town, for refusing even the buckled ends
of harness reins raising long welts
across their backs lathered by sweat
and rain, for allowing us to grab
their tails, for leading us like blind
children away from the wagon
perched on the edge of the swamp—

Father comes, opens the gate.
Bald face moves first, walking
to the biggest pumpkin, lowering
himself to his knees, placing
his broad forehead on top, using
his weight to crack the rind. Still
kneeling, he scoops the mealy flesh
into his mouth, chewing, while the other

oxen watch us, soft-jawed. Father
and I begin our dance, stomping

up and down the rows, crushing the sweet
orange spheres with our boots, and now
they all begin to feed, bending down,
rising up to gaze past the barn
where the yokes, shares, and coulters hang clean
and sharp, past the road to town
over swamps now bridged with sedge sod
tough enough to hold their weight
and the wagons, up and down, lowering
and lifting their heads, bowing to the fields.

# ARMISTICE

Not far from San Diego

steel ship containers packed with jeeps sit unopened

and someone I know very well
stands on the boulevard, surrounded by the pink
and white stucco walls
outside my window

suspended in this moment between breathing out and breathing in

the men and women at Camp Pendleton relax their arms
and listen

to the high tide covering the frayed and jagged edges
disappearing

off the docks, overwhelmed
by waves breaking on the girders, pushing
from the shore into the sea

the street dog trembles for the clear
water in the coffee can

the pigeon's up-bent wings embrace another gust

horses race across the field
legs wrapped in blurs of red, blue, yellow, kelly green


just back from overseas, my love
takes off his olive coat
unclips the holster strap
slips it off
and rests his lovely hands on his hips


fuchsia, hibiscus, bougainvillea, lantana, guava,
mango, bird of paradise


the footsteps on the stairs


dear welcome voice!
dear God, the graceful angles of your face unchanged!


listen


to the sea dissolving into the sky
at the horizon, mist curving
into the lath-moon bay, arced walls
of water encircling the city and its ships.

# DISTANT CITIES

I left. But the dawn light
all day in December,
the stretch of the Tanana Valley and then Denali,
the bent-winged bombers on maneuver
skimming the tops of trees,
the wall of cold,
and the smothering of mosquitoes
won't leave me.
Our biplane entered the mist split by spruce
and landed
in February in air that didn't hurt.
We stepped outside
and walked into a muggy June afternoon
near the lake, surrounded by thick brush—
there were no droning clouds,
despite the nagging
when will they descend? What's wrong?
What if some people are right
that discomfort, longing, itch, and cold
are gifts allowing each one of us
to focus
like a lens collecting light
above a pile of dry moss,
the glass burn by which a fire is born?
January. 60 below. Goldstream Valley.
The slightest creak carried in from far away.
Then the silence, endless—
I'm grateful to be interrupted
by the low hum of the chain saw,
the raven's craunch,
the dog team's howl, miles away

across that expanse of white,
that space—
and the night with its sky like a black field
hung with fog, swirled
fluorescent, as green as the eyes of an animal startled
and the Fort Eielson lights streaking upwards
as if the air were a cold, hard thumb
pressing each beam
down to the ground in columns,
drawing each ray up,
as if we were driving
towards a city built of soft pillars of light.

# STORM

Snowsuited, sitting perfectly still

    puffed up like a ptarmigan

        you gather with your eyes each
wind-

  ribbed drift, milkweed pod, foxtail,

    broken stem

of pampas

grass, star-spiked shadow, and pine clump

    strewn by the storm last night sweeping

      from the mountains to the sea,

cold

    wind twisting the apple tree outside

        the room where you

lay motionless

    in my arms for days, too listless

      to lift your head to drink

until the wind

knocked wires down, bowed our fence,

and your fever broke, releasing

us to sit, quelled, in the silent

after-
          storm, tipsy with delight at every icy

twig, reaching towards the shiny red

branch pointing up at the sun, tarnished

silver in the smoke-bundled sky

and suddenly

you commando crawl away from me,

grinning, rolling on your back,

flailing,

              sweeping the new green grass clean,

kicking

                             wafts of powder

up, stirring

                the effervescent, unstoppable,

      churning

flurry of which you are the center,

    as the sun lifts from the mist,

burnished

                  by strips of fog, you

kneel on your wing-marked ground, wave one

fist, press the snow—

       gritty melt of garden dirt and

crumbled leaves—

             into your mouth, laughing,

    offering me some, too.

# NOTES

"Kantishna Terns" takes place on the Kantishna River, Alaska, in July 1985.

"John Muir Remembers Eliza Hendricks" is one of several poems inspired by the life of the naturalist John Muir.

"Bodhisattva" is dedicated to the seated Kuan Yin, a lacquered wood Bodhisattva from the Sung Dynasty in the Seattle Art Museum.

"Near Nenana" occurs where the Tanana and Nenana Rivers converge.

For "Dear Hippopotamus" I wish to thank my parents, Walter and Ann Balk.

"Dusk Choir" was triggered by an incident in John Muir's childhood.

"Tonga Ridge" is dedicated to Mrs. Harriet Flaccus.

"Separation" is dedicated to Mandy, 1980.

"Shorthorns" was also inspired by John Muir's life.

"Slowly, Turning Each Edge Under" is dedicated to the Indiana quilter who signed her work "Amanda" in the late 1800s.

This book was printed on Glatfelter paper in an edition of 1,200 copies and designed by Chiquita Babb using the Centaur typeface. Centaur was created by the noted book designer Bruce Rogers (1870–1957) and modeled after the roman face of Nicholas Jenson's *Eusebius* of 1470. The face was named after the translation of *Le Centaure,* the text for which it first demonstrated its elegance and clean lines. The italic is based on the Arrighi italic of Frederic Warde.